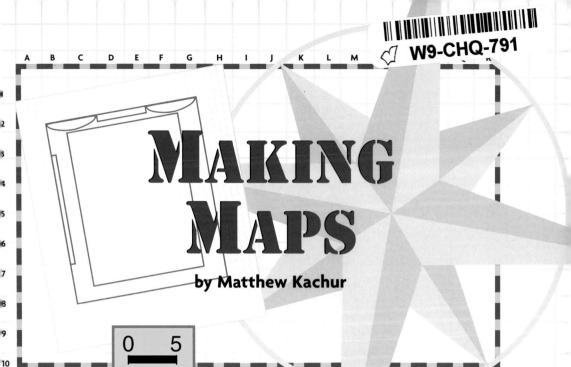

MAKING MAPS

by Matthew Kachur

Table of Contents

Introduction

"Are we there yet? Are we there yet?"

How many times have you heard someone ask that question during a car ride or a bus trip? Perhaps you've said it a few times yourself! One way to find out if you're "there yet" is to look at a map.

A **map** is a special drawing of an area that shows information about that area. A road map, for example, shows the cities, towns, streets, roads, and highways in a specific region. If you're on a trip, you can look at a road map to find out how far you are from your destination.

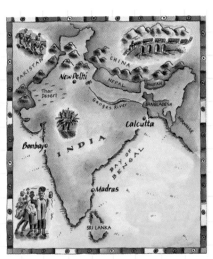
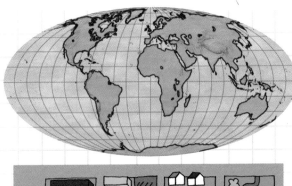

Maps can show the world, features of countries of the world, or a neighborhood.

People use maps every day. Right now, people are using road maps to find out how to get from place to place. Students are using political and historical maps to learn about places and events. Hikers are using maps that show the height of the land in a particular area. Someone in a mall is checking a sign that shows where stores are located. These signs, called mall directories, are a type of map.

In the pages that follow, you'll learn about several kinds of maps and the features that are common to all. You won't just be learning, however. You'll be making maps of your own!

This satellite map uses different colors to show weather conditions.

✓ Point

Think It Over

How much do you know about maps already? List the kinds of maps you've seen or used in the past. Identify the kinds of information you found on each.

The earliest maps that have been found are about 4,500 years old. They are preserved clay tablets. The pictures show villages and fields with geographical features, such as rivers and hills.

The first sophisticated maps came from the ancient Greeks. They mapped parts of Europe, Asia, and Africa, as well as their region in the Mediterranean. During the Middle Ages, Arab and Chinese mapmakers produced maps of the world as they knew it. Since the 1500s, new instruments for navigation and measurement have led to more accurate maps.

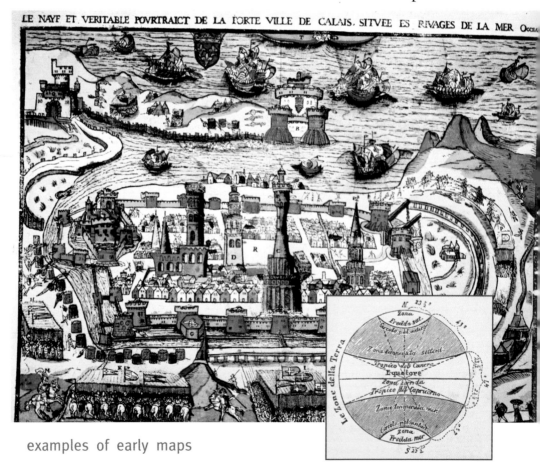

examples of early maps

Different kinds of maps present information about different topics. However, some features appear in most maps. The most common map features are:

- **scale:** the relationship between a distance on a map and the actual distance

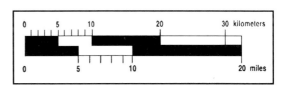

- **symbols** and **keys:** pictures that represent information on a map

- **coordinates**: a system that locates things on a map in a grid

- **relief:** the height of land as shown on a map

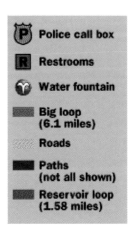

P Police call box

R Restrooms

Y Water fountain

Big loop (6.1 miles)

Roads

Paths (not all shown)

Reservoir loop (1.58 miles)

It's a Fact!

The first maps were made by early humans who simply drew lines in dirt. Today, computers, satellites, and other devices have made mapmaking a high-tech enterprise.

Map Scale

Have you heard the phrase, "a bird's-eye view"? It means a view from above, from the perspective of a bird. Most maps are bird's-eye views of things.

Picture yourself on a city sidewalk. Think about the view you have. Now imagine that you are a bird flying high above the city. What view do you have now? How is it different from your street-level view? The bird's-eye view is the key to understanding and making maps.

Notice how a view from above is different from a view at street level. The view from above can be translated onto a flat surface and made into a map.

Obviously, things on a map aren't shown in their true size. If they were, a map of the United States would have to be as big as—well, as big as the United States! That's why maps are drawn to scale.

What is "to scale"? Imagine a road map that shows a highway connecting two cities. The actual distance between the two cities is 10 miles. The mapmaker decides that on that map, one mile will be measured as one-half inch. This means that for that map, the scale is one mile equals one-half inch. So the section of highway between the two cities would be five inches.

Mapmakers show the scale of a map with a scale bar. The scale bar can usually be found toward the bottom corner of the map.

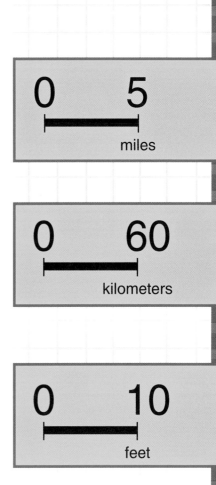

These examples of scale bars indicate how the mapmaker has decided to represent actual distances.

One way to work with a map scale is to make a map-scale strip. To make a map-scale strip, place a strip of paper along the scale bar. With a pencil or marker, transfer the measurements on the bar to the strip of paper.

To measure distances on the map, place the strip between the two locations whose distance you are measuring. Count the markings on the strip.

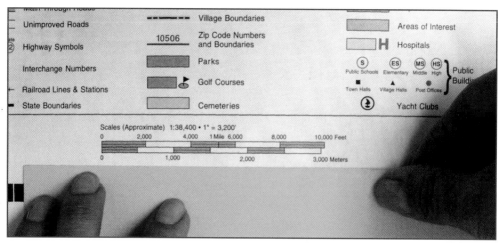

What is the scale of this road map?

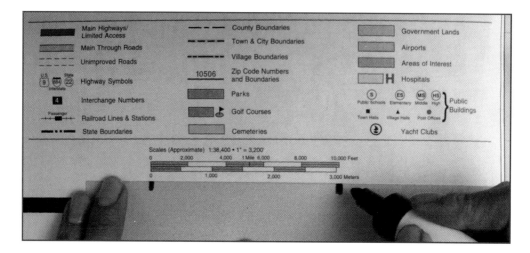

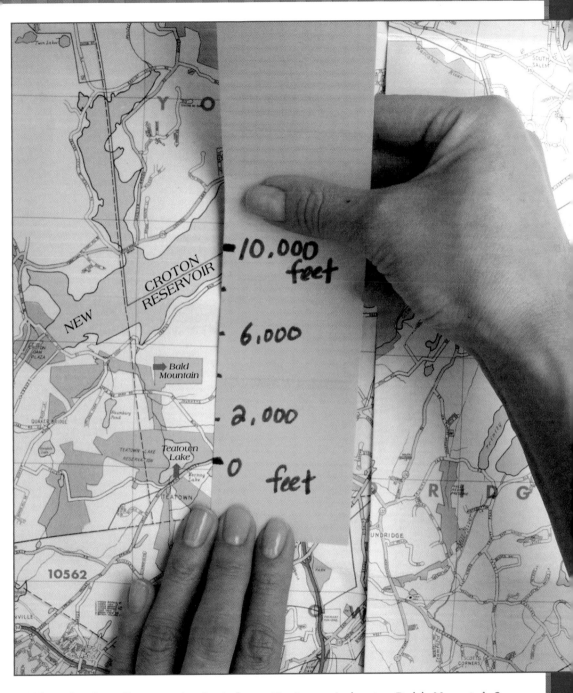

What is the distance in feet from Teatown Lake to Bald Mountain? In miles? Where would you be if you traveled 10,000 feet north of Teatown Lake?

Now it's your turn to make a map to a particular scale.

For all the mapmaking activities in this book,

YOU WILL NEED:
- graph paper
- ruler
- sharp pencil

What to do:

1. Choose a room to map. It might be a room in your home or school. Picture the room from a bird's-eye view.

2. Measure the room in footsteps. Walk the length and width of the room, counting the steps in each direction. When walking, put one foot directly in front of the other, heel to toe. Record your footsteps for the length and width. One footstep will equal one square on the graph paper.

3. On the graph paper, draw your room. Remember, each measurement will use the scale 1 footstep = 1 square.

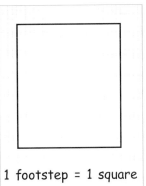

1 footstep = 1 square

4. Measure the width of the doors in footsteps and add them to the map according to the scale. Do the same for the windows.

5. Use the scale to measure large pieces of furniture, such as beds, desks, and cabinets, and add them to the map.

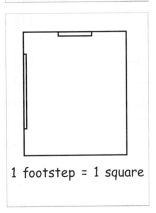

1 footstep = 1 square

6. Label each item on your map to identify it.

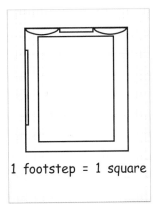

1 footstep = 1 square

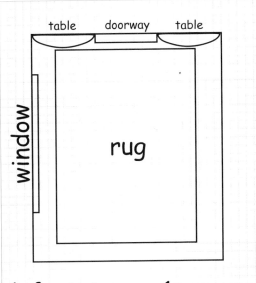

table   doorway   table

window

rug

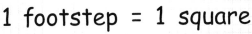

1 footstep = 1 square

Map Symbols and Keys

The map you made of a room is fairly simple. Everything on it has a label. Other maps are more complicated. They contain a lot of information in a small space. These maps often use symbols.

A symbol is generally a number, letter, line, dot, color, or small picture that represents something else. For example, a highway on a road map doesn't look like a real highway. Instead, a line of a certain thickness and color stands for a highway. To indicate what the symbols mean, a key is included. The key shows each symbol along with a short explanation of what it represents. The key is usually in a small box.

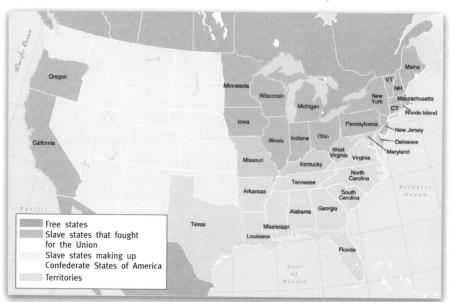

This map shows the states on the eve of the Civil War. The key explains what the colors mean.

Look at the maps on this page. The map keys have been left off! Can you guess what kind of information is being presented in each map?

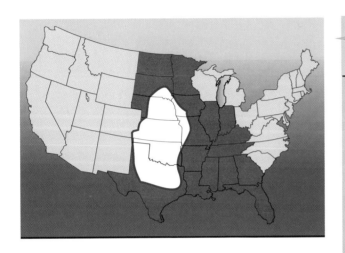

Atlantic Ocean

Pacific Ocean

Look at Map Sense on page 30 for the answers.

It's a Fact!

One important symbol that you will find on just about every map is the **compass rose.** A compass rose is usually a four-pointed star that shows where north, south, east, and west are on the map.

A product map shows what is grown or made in a particular area. On the opposite page is a blank outline map of Indiana. Your job is to make a product map of the state.

What to do:

1. Trace the outline of the map on a sheet of paper.

2. Draw symbols on the map to show each of the following facts. Decide what symbols to use.

   • Indianapolis is the state capital. Evansville and Gary are other cities in Indiana.

   • The area southeast of Gary is known for its dairy products.

   • Manufacturing is important around Indianapolis.

   • Wheat is grown north of Evansville.

   • Corn is grown in the northeast corner of the state.

3. Get a map of your state to trace. Find out what products are grown or made in particular areas. Make a product map of your state. Remember to include the state capital.

PRODUCT MAP OF INDIANA

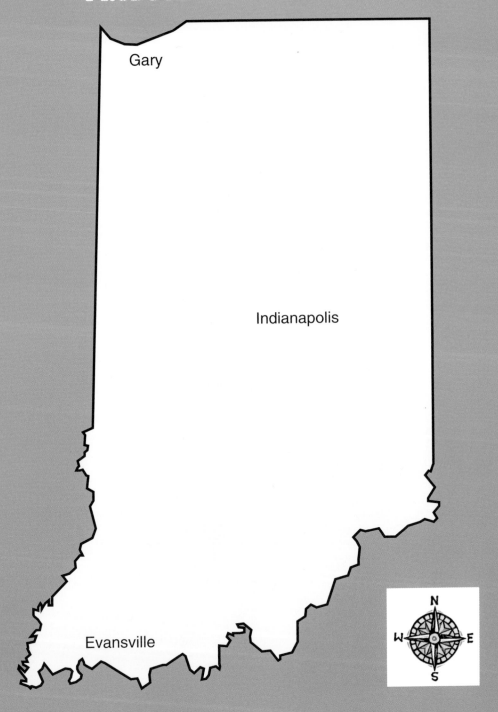

Gary

Indianapolis

Evansville

In this activity, you will make a neighborhood map. You will use a particular scale and include symbols for a variety of things.

What to do:

1. First, decide what area you would like to map. Don't choose an area that is too big. Don't try to map your entire town or city—not yet, anyway! Choose a smaller area, such as your neighborhood.

2. Imagine the area from a bird's-eye view. Make a sketch of your map.

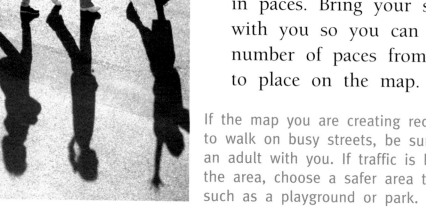

3. Walk around the area you are mapping, measuring distances in paces. Bring your sketch with you so you can note the number of paces from place to place on the map.

If the map you are creating requires you to walk on busy streets, be sure to have an adult with you. If traffic is heavy in the area, choose a safer area to map, such as a playground or park.

4. Take note of the special features of the area you are mapping. Is there a firehouse? A park? Stores? Schools?

5. When you've finished your pacing and note-taking, create your final map on graph paper.

6. Take 10 paces and measure the distance you cover. Translate your pace numbers into actual measurements and add a scale bar to your map.

7. Create symbols for the special features of the area and draw them on your map. Don't forget a map key and a compass rose!

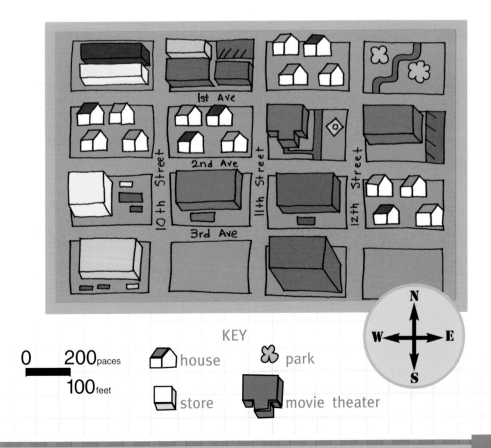

Map Coordinates

A map is not very helpful if you can't find the information you need. To make information easier to find, maps are often divided into squares. The squares are drawn with faint lines so that they don't interfere with the contents of the map. The squares are called **grid squares.**

The columns and rows of grid squares have corresponding letters and numbers called coordinates. For example, the columns of squares might be A, B, C, etc. The rows might be 1, 2, 3, etc.

Suppose you know that a location or feature you are looking for is in grid square B2. You first find the column labeled B and the row marked 2 and then you run your finger down and across. What you're looking for will be in that square.

This family will locate a point of interest by using map coordinates and grid squares.

Look at the map below. A student very much like you made it, following the instructions in the previous chapter. The student added grid lines to the map, along with coordinates at the top and bottom, and the left and right.

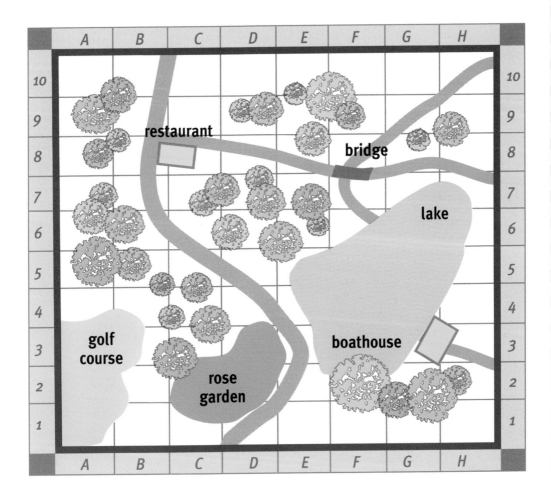

The grid lines and coordinates make locating places on a map much easier. How would you describe the locations of the six places shown on the map?

Below is a treasure map showing an island with several landmarks. Landmarks identify specific places on a map. According to this map, what is located in grid square C4? In which grid square is Wolf Rock located? In which grid square is the Hidden Forest located? Some things on a map appear in more than one grid square. In which two grid squares does Good Luck Lake appear?

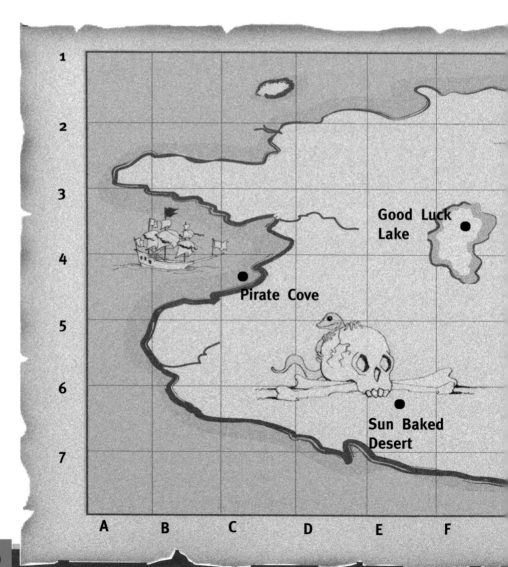

Map coordinates are useful for all kinds of maps, but they are especially important for road maps and city maps. People use the coordinates on those maps to find specific streets, locations, or features of interest.

In the activity on page 22, you will use your imagination to make a map that has a scale, symbols to stand for special places, and coordinates that make it easy to use.

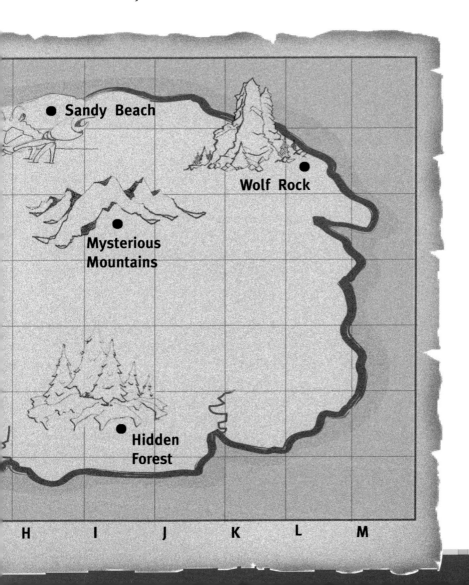

What to do:

1. Think of a place you would like to map.

2. Using graph paper, sketch the details of your map. Include as many features as possible. If you are creating a city street map, name your streets and include symbols for places such as schools, parks, museums, famous buildings, or hospitals. If you are creating a map of a park, include all the things you would find there, using symbols as appropriate.

It's a Fact!

The world has been divided into a grid of imaginary lines called lines of **latitude** and lines of **longitude.** Lines of longitude run north and south from pole to pole. Lines of latitude run around the globe, parallel to the equator. Lines of latitude and longitude are measured in units called degrees.

3. When you have finished your map, create grid lines using a ruler and the lines on the graph paper. Add letters across the top and bottom, and numbers running down the sides.

4. At the bottom of your map, make a list of the main features of the site. Next to the name of each feature, give its grid coordinates. Exchange maps with a friend and use your grids to find features.

✓ Point

Talk About It

Before beginning your map, talk to a group member about what you want to draw. Maybe he or she has suggestions for you.

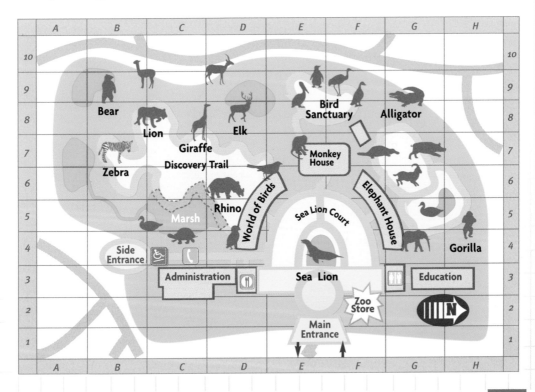

Relief Maps

Have you ever heard the expression, "the lay of the land"? This phrase refers to the actual physical landscape of an area—its mountains, valleys, hills, or plains. Geographers call the physical characteristics of an area the **topography** or relief.

There are several ways a map can show the height of the land and how steeply it rises or falls. The maps on page 25 are two examples. Although maps are flat and Earth's surface isn't, that hasn't stopped mapmakers from representing the information.

On a topographical, or relief, map, the heights of all the land features in this photo would be represented.

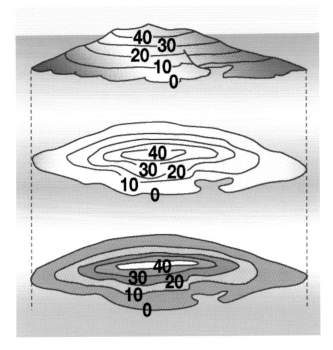

A contour map has lines called **contours** that join places on the map that are the same height. If the contour lines are close together, the land is steep. If the contour lines are far apart, the land is sloping more gradually.

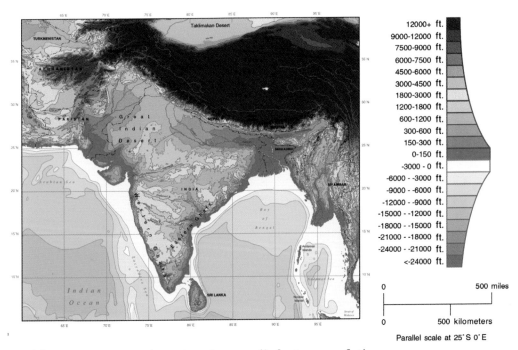

This map uses colors to show relief. Areas of the same height are given the same color. The map key shows the range of heights for each color.

This activity will give you hands-on experience with the way contour maps are made.

WHAT YOU NEED:

sand
large, square, wooden board
pencil
ruler
colored yarn of several different colors
large piece of chart paper

What to do:

1. Dampen the sand slightly.

2. On the wooden board, build a hill out of some damp sand.

3. Push the pencil point into the sand to make a series of rows of holes around the hill. Use a ruler to carefully make each row the same height all the way around.

4. Lay lengths of yarn around the hill to join each row of holes. Use a different color for each row.

5. Look down—with a bird's-eye view—on your hill. The lines of yarn will look like the contours on the contour map on page 25.

6. Carefully draw the lines onto the piece of chart paper to make your contour map.

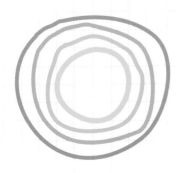

How did your contour-map hill come out? Maybe you'd like to make your hill part of a color-symbol relief map that shows a larger area. Look back at the relief map on page 25. Could you translate your contour map into a relief map like that?

Can you think of any more features you would like to locate on a map? What symbols would you use to identify these features? Below are some commonly used symbols on relief maps. Perhaps you can put them on your map.

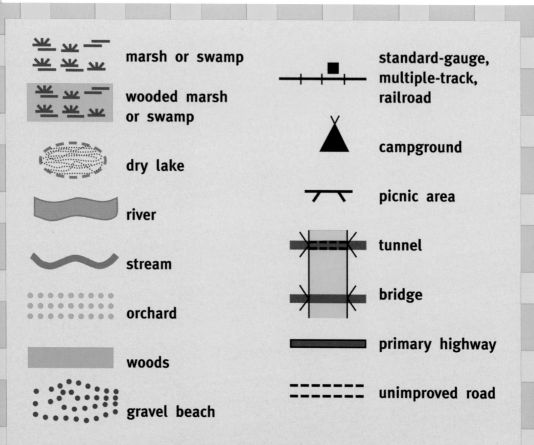

marsh or swamp

wooded marsh or swamp

dry lake

river

stream

orchard

woods

gravel beach

standard-gauge, multiple-track, railroad

campground

picnic area

tunnel

bridge

primary highway

unimproved road

Did you know that more than 70 percent of the surface of Earth is covered by water? There's a lot of land under that water to be mapped, and geographers are busy mapping it.

Mapmakers have developed ways to send sound waves into the water and measure their echoes. They then analyze the measurements and translate the information into a map that shows the topography of the ocean floor.

Point

Read More About It

Using reference materials, determine how oceanographers map the ocean floor. Write the steps on a sheet of paper.

By analyzing underwater measurements, mapmakers create maps of the ocean floor.

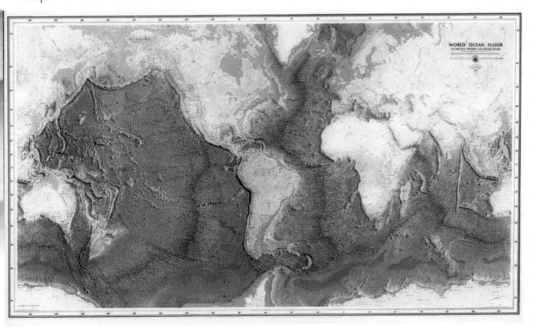

WORLD OCEAN FLOOR

MAP SENSE

Using the key for each map, describe what information the maps provide.

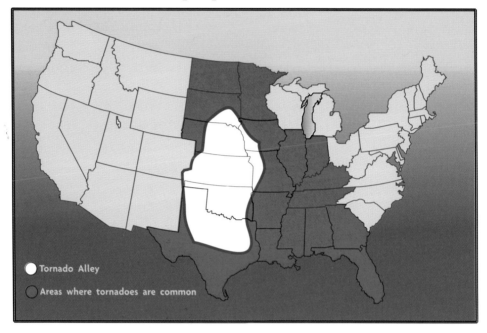

Tornado Alley

Areas where tornadoes are common

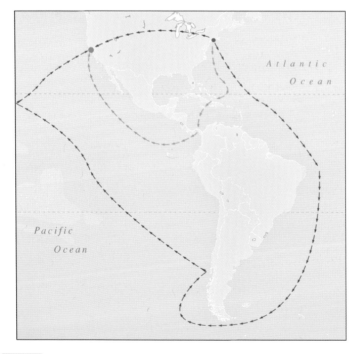

Atlantic
Ocean

Pacific
Ocean

South America route

Panama route

land route

Glossary

compass rose	(KUHM-pehss ROSE) a symbol on a map that shows direction (page 13)
contour	(KAHN-tor) a line on a map that shows the height of the land (page 25)
coordinate	(cuh-WOR-dih-niht) a number and a letter that match a layout that divides a map into squares, making things on the map easier to find (page 5)
grid square	(GRIHD SKWEAR) a square drawn on a map that reflects the map coordinates (page 18)
key	(KEE) an explanation of the symbols on a map (page 5)
latitude	(LAT-ih-tood) the distance north or south of the equator, measured in degrees (page 22)
longitude	(LONJ-ih-tood) the distance east or west of the Prime Meridian, measured in degrees (page 22)
map	(MAP) a special drawing of an area that shows information about that area (page 2)
relief	(ruh-LEEF) the height of the land shown on a map (page 5)
scale	(SKAYL) the relationship between the distance shown on a map and the actual distance or size of what is being shown (page 5)
symbol	(SIM-buhl) a picture that represents information on a map (page 5)
topography	(TUH-pog-ruh-fee) the physical landscape of an area (page 24)

Index